# JavaScript for Kids

## Start Your Coding Adventure

Abdelfattah Ragab

# JavaScript for Kids

Start Your Coding Adventure

Abdelfattah Ragab

# Introduction

Welcome to the book "JavaScript for Kids: Start your Coding Adventure".
This book is your introduction to the world of JavaScript. It's your first step towards developing websites and mobile applications. With JavaScript, you can turn your ideas into reality. Learning should be fun, so you will feel like you are reading a story.
By the end of this book, you will have a good understanding of JavaScript. You will have taken the first steps in your modern web programming adventure.
Have fun programming!

# Move forward

When you start a new topic, you should explore it broadly and focus on moving forward without getting lost in the details. I also recommend that you gather information on the same topic from different sources. Take breaks from time to time, look for short answers to questions, and use different sources to get different perspectives. Don´t worry if you still don't understand after many attempts, just keep going because you will come across it again later.

# Java vs JavaScript

Java and JavaScript are different programming languages with different goals: Java is a general-purpose, object-oriented language used for developing applications for various platforms, while JavaScript is a scripting language used mainly for creating interactive content on websites.

# What is JavaScript?

JavaScript is a programming language that is mainly used to create interactive content on websites. It allows developers to implement features on web pages, such as interactive forms and real-time updates, without having to reload the page.

JavaScript was primarily developed for execution by the web browser. You are familiar with web browsers because we use them all the time. The most popular browsers include Google Chrome, Microsoft Edge, Mozilla Firefox, Opera and Safari.

JavaScript is a programming language that mainly exists and is executed within the web browser. This was the case for many years before the release of Node.js. With Node.js, you can use JavaScript for server-side programming outside the web browser. Now we use JavaScript for all types of programming.

# How do web browsers work?

When you visit a website in the browser, it goes to the specified URL, downloads the files and displays them on the screen. Websites are made up of three types of files that together make up the page you see online.
First, there is the HTML code, which is responsible for the content of the website, with no styles or programming, just the content.
Let's say we have a web page for a product on Amazon.com. The HTML consists of the product name, price, images, description and shipping details.
Everything is written in plain text, line by line. And the images are displayed one after the other, each on a separate line.
Imagine I give you some information and ask you to write it down in your notebook.
You write the product name on the first line, the price on the second line and so on.
Just the information without any design or programming.

That's what HTML does: it displays the information in a semantic way. Accessibility devices read their information from the HTML. They are mainly interested in the information. If you use a screen reader for a blind user, it will read the content of the page. All styles are ignored.

However, for sighted people who can see and interact with the website, the styles are important.

For example, if we apply styles to a product page on Amazon, we can make the title bigger and put the images on the left-hand side in a separate area. We can also hide all the images and only show the first image in a carousel or slider. We can change colors, fonts, spacing and borders, draw shapes and do all sorts of things with CSS.

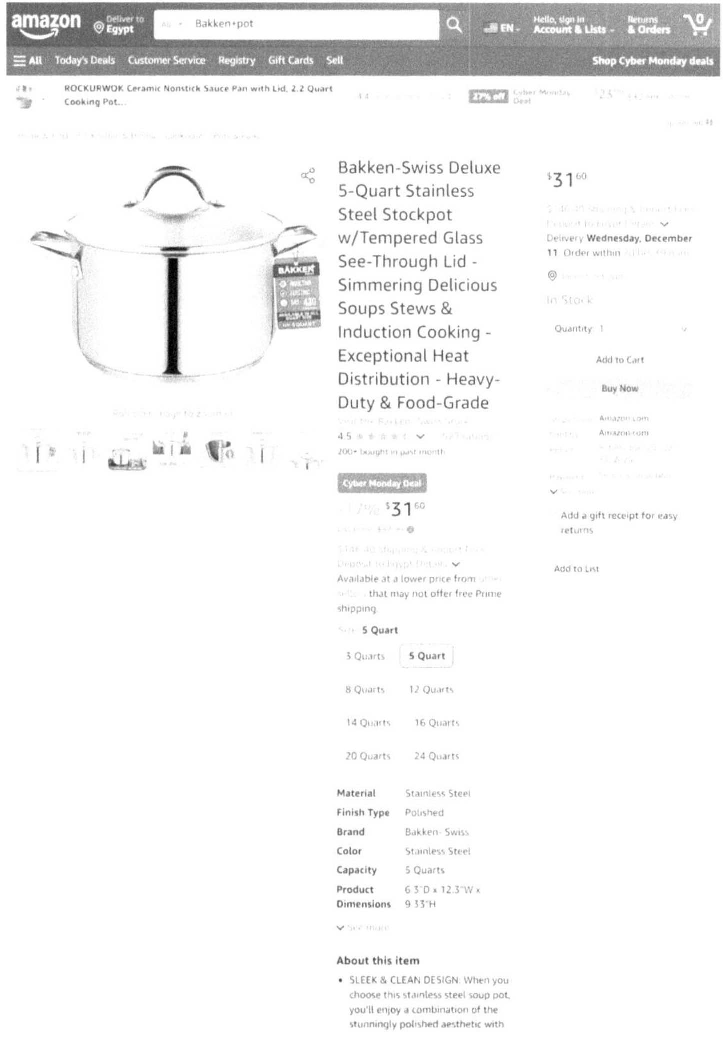



So, now you know HTML and CSS, but there's a third component: JavaScript.

# What is programming?

Programming is the process of creating a set of instructions that a computer can follow to perform specific tasks.

# Create a small application

Let us create a small application so that you understand what programming means.
The application takes two numbers and should return the sum of the two.
I will create a variable called first `firstNumber` and a second one called `secondNumber`.
You can define the variables `x` and `y`, but professional programmers recommend giving the variables a meaningful name that clarifies the purpose of the creation. This is very useful when sharing your code with others so that they can easily understand what you are trying to do.

```
let firstNumber;
let secondNumber;
return firstNumber + secondNumber;
```

In JavaScript, we use the word `let` to declare a variable. You can then refer to the variable name to perform calculations.

We use the word `return` to return the final result once the calculations are complete.
To be able to call this, it is inserted into a function.

```
function sum(firstNumber, secondNumber)
{
    return firstNumber + secondNumber;
}
```

You can then call it as follows:
```
const result = sum(1, 2);
console.log('Result is: ', result)
```

`const` is similar to `let`, but is used for constants that will not change. We can still use `let`, but we use `const` to save memory and prevent others from changing it.

`Console.log` is used to display a message in the browser console. You can display multiple values with commas in between like I did. I show the statement 'Result is: ' followed by the actual result.

# Try it yourself

Search for "online javascript compiler" and choose your favorite online JavaScript compiler.
Write the code in the online compiler and run it.
```
function sum(firstNumber, secondNumber)
{
    return firstNumber + secondNumber;
```

```javascript
}

const result = sum(1, 2);
console.log('Result is: ', result)
```

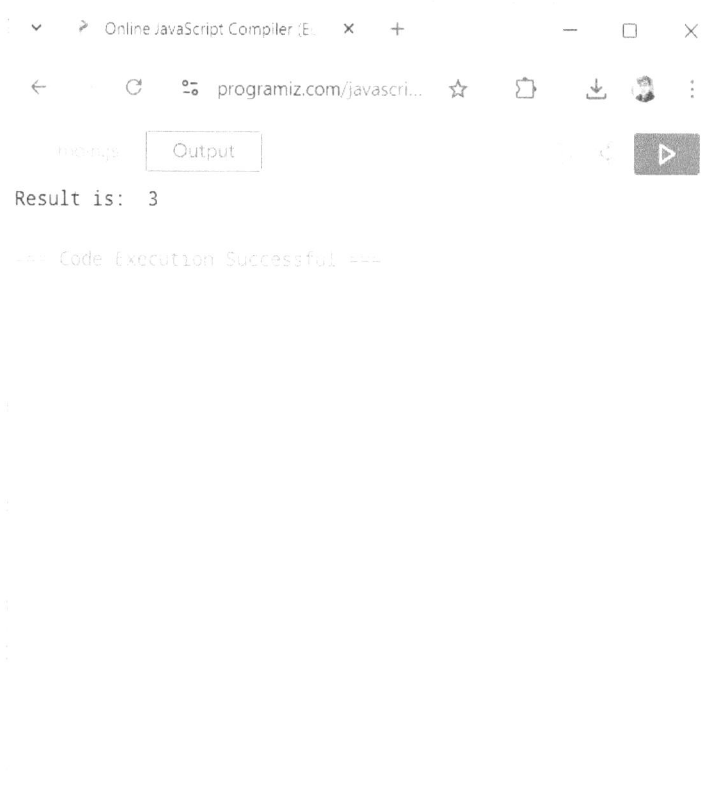



**Congratulations!** You have created your first JavaScript program. All that comes next are variations of what you have done.

# DOM (Document Object Model)

When a web page is loaded in a browser, the browser creates a DOM of the page, which is essentially a tree-like structure where each node corresponds to a part of the document, such as elements, attributes, and text.

# JavaScript and DOM

JavaScript allows you to access the dom, so you can modify the web page programmatically at run time. The browser window is represented by the window object, which you can access in JavaScript to get information about things such as location and so on. The other important object which is available for you in JavaScript is the document object, which represents the entire HTML document loaded in the browser. It provides methods to access and manipulate the content of the document.

# `document.querySelector()`

The `document.querySelector()` method is a powerful function in JavaScript that allows you to select HTML elements using CSS selectors.

The string passed to querySelector() must be a valid CSS selector. This is related to CSS, so here are some examples on CSS selectors.

Let's say you have the following HTML in your web page:

```html
<div id="myDiv" class="container">
    <p class="text">Hello, World!</p>
</div>
```

# Select element by tag name

To select the first paragraph:

```javascript
let firstParagraph =
document.querySelector("p");
```

This will select the bolded paragraph element

```html
<div id="myDiv" class="container">
    <p class="text">Hello, World!</p>
</div>
```

There is another method called `querySelectorAll`, that you can use if you want to select all the paragraphs in the document.

# Select element by id

To select the element with the id **myDiv**:

```javascript
let myDivElement =
document.querySelector("#myDiv");
```

Note the # in front of the id.
This will select the bolded div element.

```
<div id="myDiv" class="container">
    <p class="text">Hello, World!</p>
</div>
```

# Select element by class name

To select the element with the class **container**:

```
let myDivElement =
document.querySelector(".container");
```

Note the dot in front of the class name.
This will select the bolded div element.

```
<div id="myDiv" class="container">
    <p class="text">Hello, World!</p>
</div>
```

# Manipulate DOM

Once you select the element you can do anything with it.
You can read its contents, modify its properties such as
color, size etc... Or you can even delete it from the page
or do anything you like.

# Other selectors

`document.querySelector` and
`document.querySelectorAll` are new methods
that were added recently with the release of DOM Level

3 Specifications; before them there were other methods for selecting elements which are still valid for use today.

```
document.getElementById()
document.getElementsByClassName()
document.getElementsByTagName()
```

# Primitive types vs Reference types

We categorize data types into two main groups: primitive types and reference types.

**Primitive types** are the most basic data types and represent single values.

**Reference types** are more complex data types that can hold collections of values.

# Primitive types

**Number:** Represents both integer and floating-point numbers

```
let num = 42;
```

**String:** Represents a sequence of characters.

```
let str = "Hello, World!";
```

**Boolean:** Represents a logical entity and can be either true or false.

```
let isActive = true;
```

# Reference types

Reference types are more complex data structures that can hold collections of values.

**Object:** An object is a collection of key-value pairs that can store multiple values of different types and are used to represent real-world entities.

```
let person = {
    name: "Alice",
    age: 30,
    isActive: true
};
```

**Array:** An array is a special type of object that is used to store ordered collections of values. Arrays can hold elements of any type, including other arrays or objects.

```
let colors = ["red", "green", "blue"];
```

# Default value

When you declare a variable it will have the value `undefined` by default.

# Operators

Operators are special symbols that perform operations on one or more values or variables. They are fundamental to programming as they allow developers to perform calculations and control the flow of the program.

**Arithmetic Operators:**

Arithmetic operators are used to perform mathematical calculations.

- \+ : Addition.
- \- : Subtraction.
- * : Multiplication.
- / : Division.

**Comparison Operators:**

Comparison operators are used to compare two values and return a Boolean result (true or false).

- == : Equal
- != : Not Equal
- > : Greater Than
- < : Less Than

# Conditional Statements

Conditional statements control the flow of execution in your code based on specific conditions. They allow you to execute different blocks of code depending on whether a condition evaluates to `true` or `false`.

```
let score = 80;

if (score > 60) {
    console.log("You passed!");
} else {
```

```javascript
    console.log("You failed.");
}
```

The `if` statement executes a block of code if the specified condition is true.
The `else` statement executes when the condition is false.

# Ternary Operator

The ternary operator is a shorthand for the `if...else` statement.

condition **?** expression If True **:** expression If False;

```javascript
let score = 80;
const result = score > 60 ? "You
passed!" : "You failed.";
console.log(result);

// Outputs: You passed!
```

# Loops

Loops allow you to execute a block of code repeatedly based on a specified condition.

```javascript
for (let i = 0; i < 5; i++) {
    console.log(i);
}
```

```
// Outputs: 0, 1, 2, 3, 4
```

You can write loops using the `while` loop
```
let count = 0;
while (count < 5) {
    console.log(count);
    count++;
}
// Outputs: 0, 1, 2, 3, 4
```

# Events

Events are notifications that something has happened in the system. When an event occurs, it can trigger a specific reaction in your JavaScript code. For example, when a user clicks a button, an event is triggered and you can write code that executes in response to that click.
There are many types of events for the mouse (e.g. click), for the keyboard (e.g. key press), for the window (e.g. resize) and many more.

For example, we have the HTML button with the ID myButton:
```
<button id="myButton">Click Me</button>
```

We can attach an event handler to the click action using JavaScript as follows:

```javascript
const myButtonElement =
document.querySelector('#myButton');
myButtonElement.addEventListener('click',() =>
{
    console.log('Button clicked!');
});
```

# Arrow functions

Arrow functions are a concise way to write function
expressions in JavaScript, introduced in ES6. They
provide a more streamlined syntax compared to
traditional function expressions.

**Old way:**
```javascript
function sum(firstNumber, secondNumber)
{
   return firstNumber + secondNumber;
}
```

**Arrow function:**
```javascript
const sum = (firstNumber, secondNumber)
=> {
   return firstNumber + secondNumber;
}
```

They are particularly useful for writing cleaner code
when dealing with callbacks.

# Example on local machine

Now let's create a web page on your computer and have fun manipulating the DOM. We want to change the background color when the user clicks. But first we need to set up the environment.

## Visual Studio Code

Download and install Visual Studio Code.

## Live Server Extension

From the extensions tab of the Visual Studio Code, install the Live Server extension by Ritwick Dey.

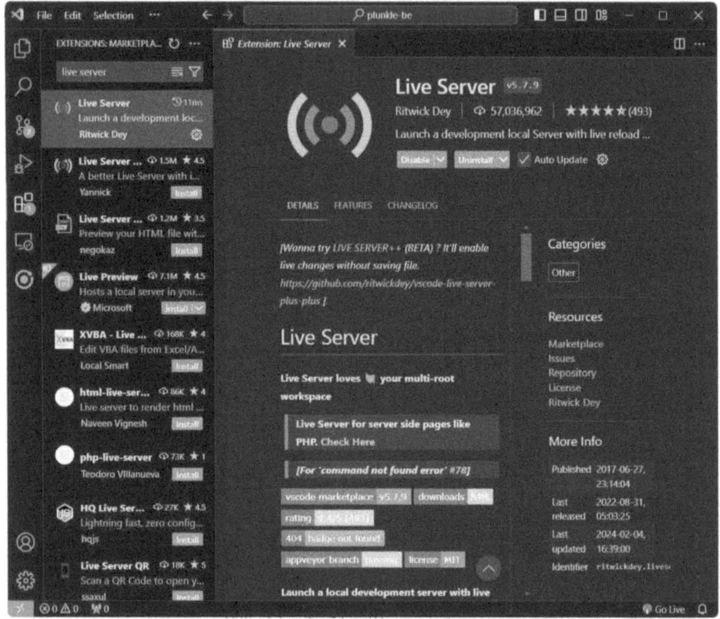

# Open Folder

From the "**File**" menu, choose "**Open Folder..**". Select the folder on your computer where you want to save your work.

# Create a new file

Create a new file and name it **index.html**

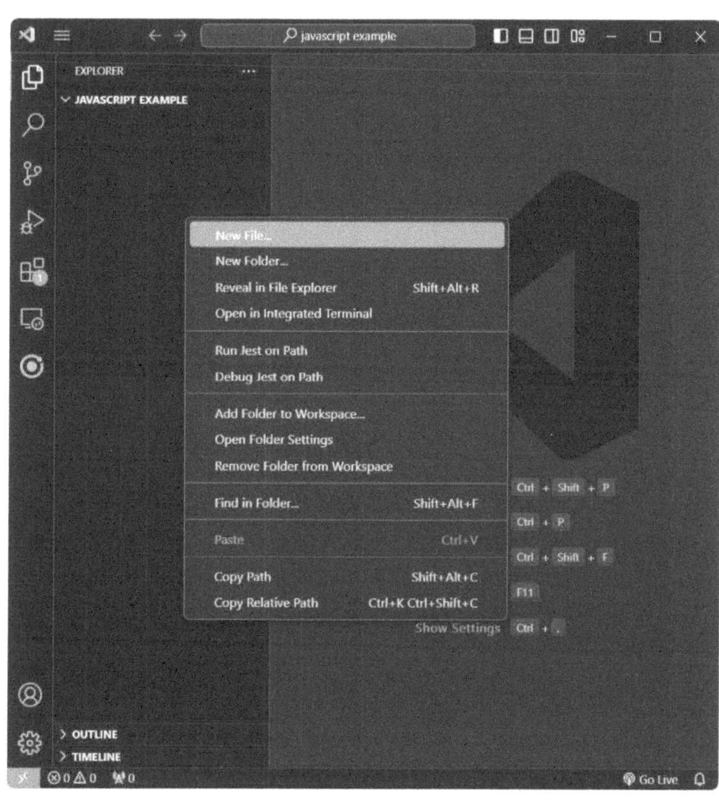
javascript example
EXPLORER
JAVASCRIPT EXAMPLE
New File...
New Folder...
Reveal in File Explorer
Shift+Alt+R
Open in Integrated Terminal
Run Jest on Path
Debug Jest on Path
Add Folder to Workspace...
Open Folder Settings
Remove Folder from Workspace
Find in Folder...
Shift+Alt+F
Paste
Ctrl+V
Copy Path
Shift+Alt+C
Copy Relative Path
Ctrl+K Ctrl+Shift+C
Ctrl + Shift + P
Ctrl + P
Ctrl + Shift + F
F11
Show Settings
Ctrl + ,
OUTLINE
TIMELINE
Go Live

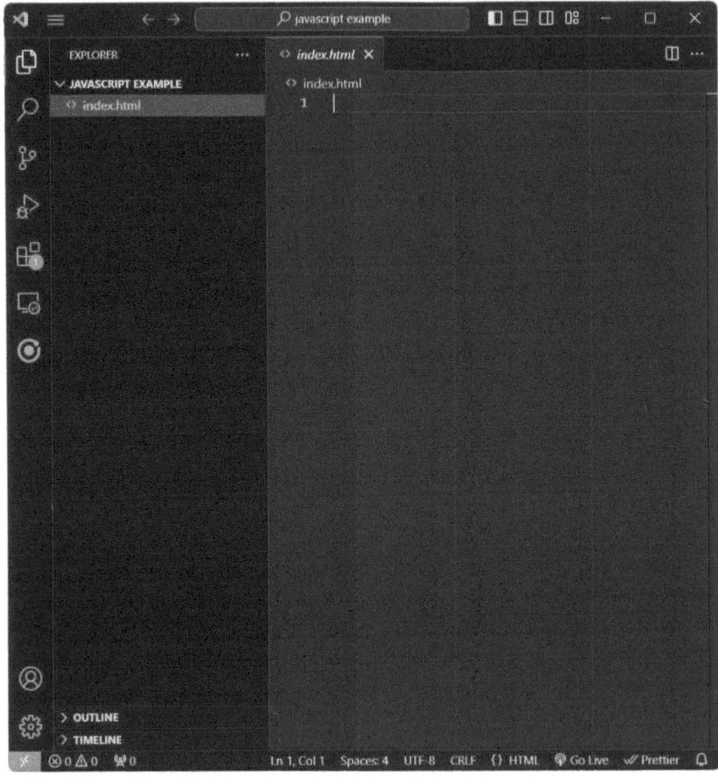

# Add HTML

Visual Studio Code helps you to create the HTML file. Start typing "html" and you will be shown some suggestions. Select the suggestion with "html:5". It will generate the HTML file for you.

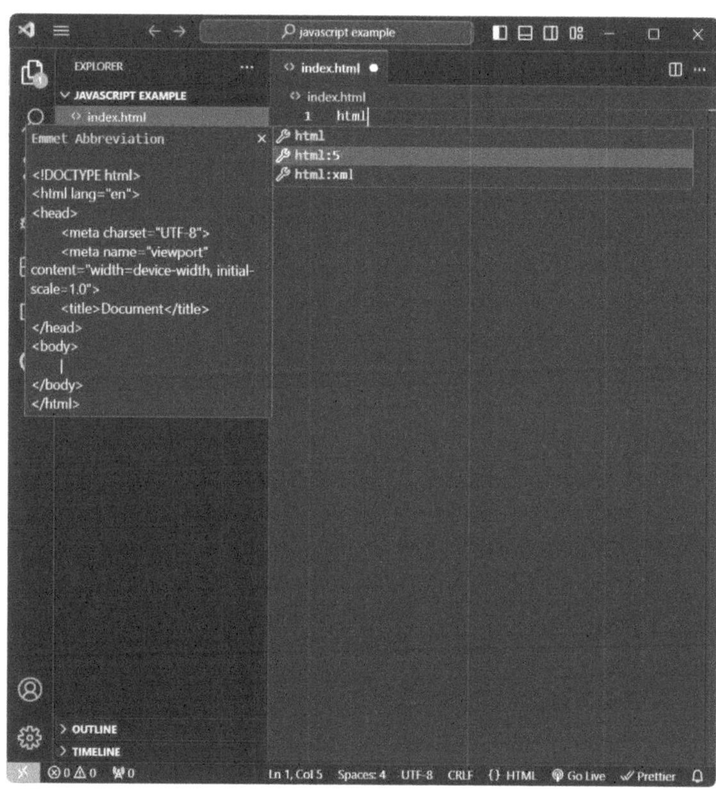

javascript example
EXPLORER
index.html
index.html
JAVASCRIPT EXAMPLE
index.html
index.html
1    html
Emmet Abbreviation                    X
html
html:5
html:xml
<!DOCTYPE html>
<html lang="en">
<head>
    <meta charset="UTF-8">
    <meta name="viewport"
content="width=device-width, initial-
scale=1.0">
    <title>Document</title>
</head>
<body>

</body>
</html>
OUTLINE
TIMELINE
0  0  0
Ln 1, Col 5    Spaces: 4    UTF-8    CRLF    {} HTML    Go Live    Prettier

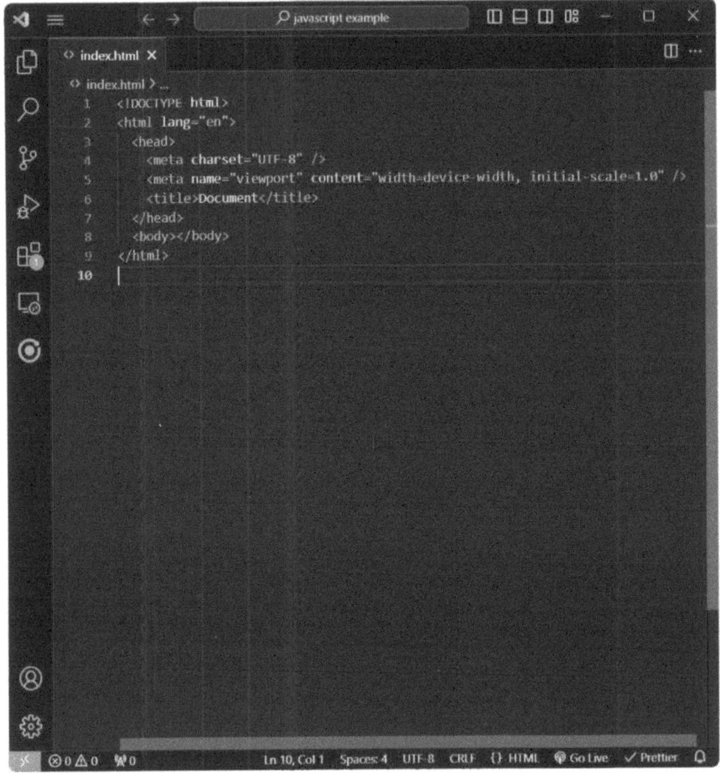

# Open in Live Server

Right click anywhere in the file and choose "**Open with Live Server**"

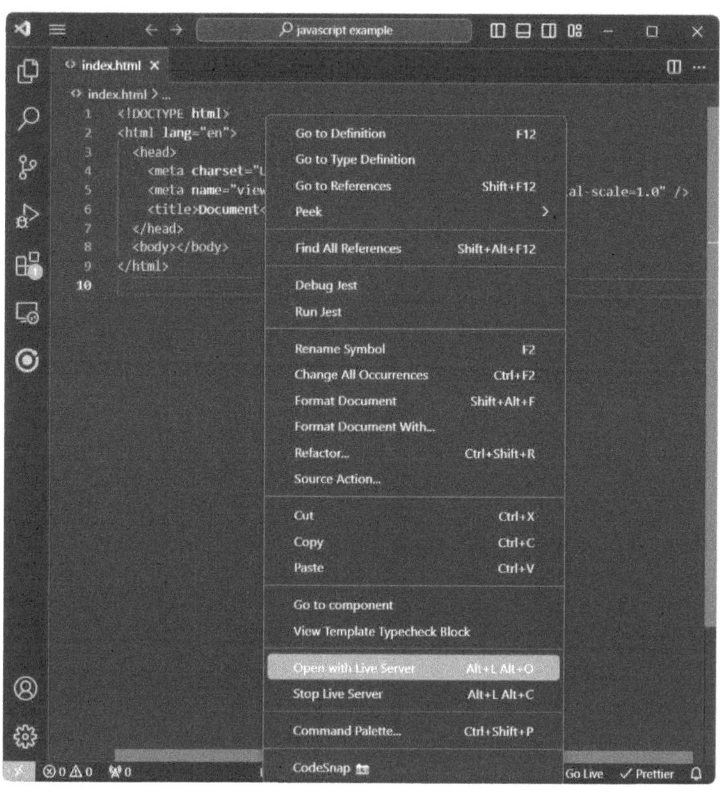
javascript example
index.html
index.html > ...
1  <!DOCTYPE html>
2  <html lang="en">
3    <head>
4      <meta charset="U
5      <meta name="view
6      <title>Document<
7    </head>
8    <body></body>
9  </html>
10
Go to Definition            F12
Go to Type Definition
Go to References            Shift+F12
Peek                             >
Find All References         Shift+Alt+F12
Debug Jest
Run Jest
Rename Symbol               F2
Change All Occurrences     Ctrl+F2
Format Document            Shift+Alt+F
Format Document With...
Refactor...                    Ctrl+Shift+R
Source Action...
Cut                             Ctrl+X
Copy                           Ctrl+C
Paste                          Ctrl+V
Go to component
View Template Typecheck Block
Open with Live Server       Alt+L Alt+O
Stop Live Server            Alt+L Alt+C
Command Palette...          Ctrl+Shift+P
CodeSnap
Go Live    Prettier

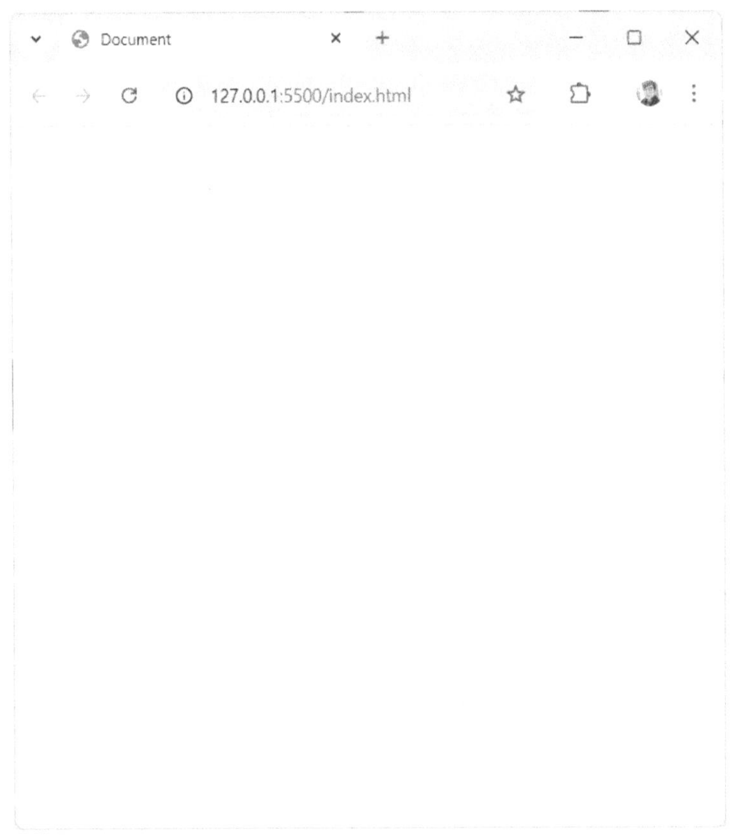

# Change the title

Change the title from "*Document*" to "*JavaScript Example*"

```
<!DOCTYPE html>
<html lang="en">
  <head>
    <meta charset="UTF-8" />
```

```html
    <meta name="viewport"
content="width=device-width, initial-scale=1.0"
/>
    <title>JavaScript Example</title>
  </head>
  <body></body>
</html>
```

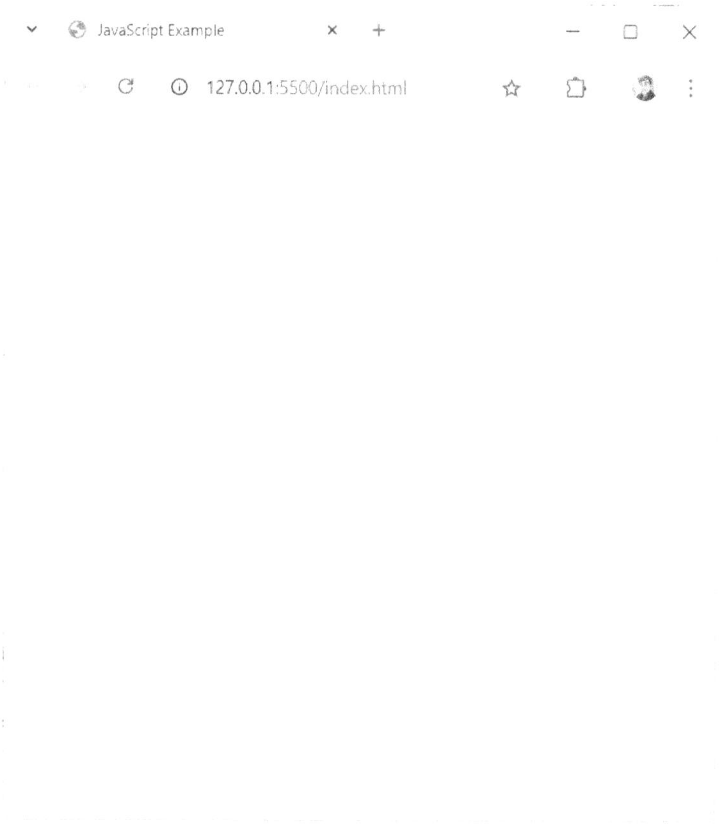

# Internal scripts

You can place your JavaScript code within a `<script>` tag in the HTML document. This method is suitable for small scripts.

```html
<!DOCTYPE html>
<html lang="en">
  <head>
    <meta charset="UTF-8" />
    <meta name="viewport"
content="width=device-width, initial-scale=1.0"
/>
    <title>JavaScript Example</title>
  </head>
  <body></body>
  <script>
    console.log("Hello!");
  </script>
</html>
```

# External scripts

For larger scripts or when you want to reuse code across multiple HTML files, it's best to use an external JavaScript file.

# Create scripts.js file

Crate another file **scripts.js**

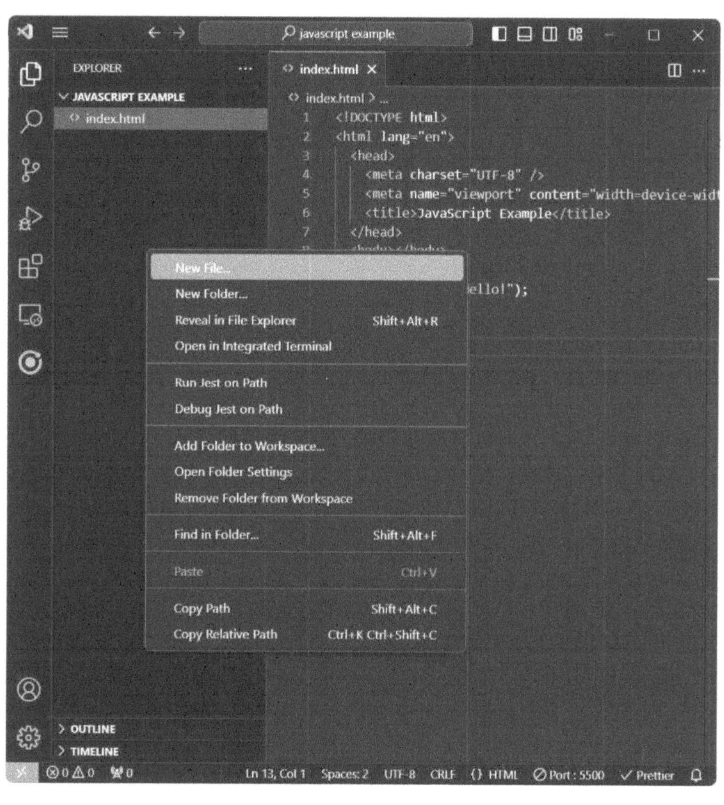

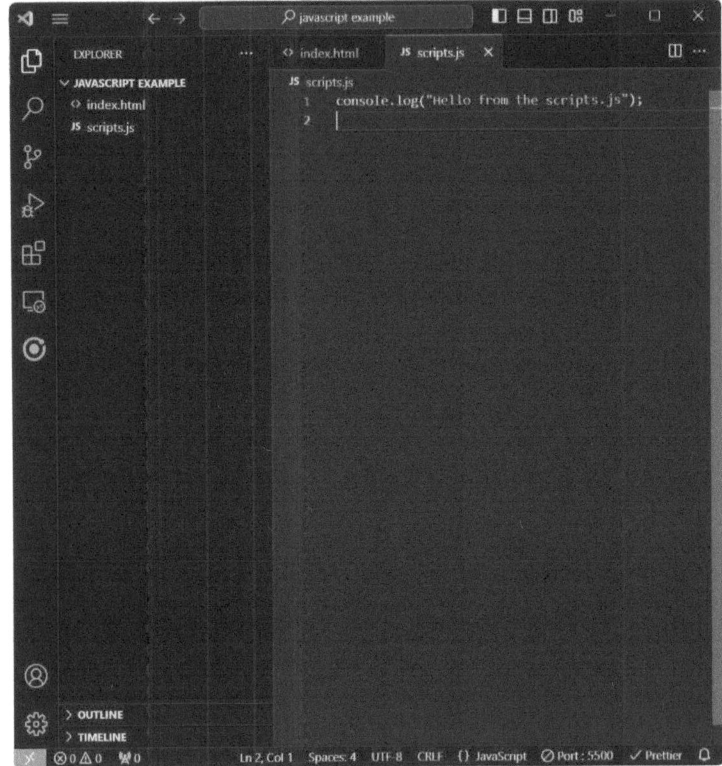

Add a console log line as follows:

```
console.log("Hello from the scripts.js");
```

# Link it to the index.html

Add the `script` tag to the html page and set the `src`
attribute to point to the scripts file as follows:

```
<!DOCTYPE html>
<html lang="en">
  <head>
```

```html
    <meta charset="UTF-8" />
    <meta name="viewport"
content="width=device-width, initial-scale=1.0"
/>
    <title>JavaScript Example</title>
    <script src="scripts.js"></script>
  </head>
  <body></body>
</html>
```

# Dev Tools

`console.log` messages are displayed in the browser console. Open the dev tools and go to the console tab to read the console log messages.

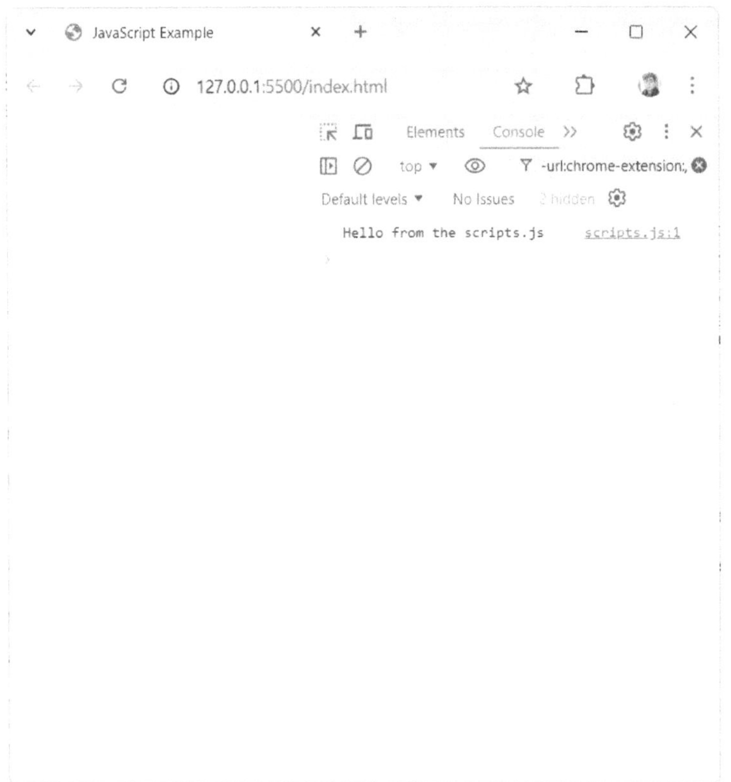


# Change background color upon click

Add the following html to your **index.html** file inside the `<body>` tag.

```
<button id="myButton">Colorize</button>
<div
  id="myDiv"
```

```
    style="width: 300px; height: 200px;
background-color: red"
></div>
```

**Add the script as follows:**

```
<script>
  const myButton =
document.querySelector("#myButton");
  myButton.addEventListener("click", () => {
    const myDiv =
document.querySelector("#myDiv");
    myDiv.style.backgroundColor = "green";
  });
</script>
```

Here is the full code, the complete html file. You can copy/paste it into the index.html file and start the live server to see it in action.

```
<!DOCTYPE html>
<html lang="en">
  <head>
    <meta charset="UTF-8" />
    <meta name="viewport"
content="width=device-width, initial-scale=1.0"
/>
    <title>JavaScript Example</title>
    <script src="scripts.js"></script>
  </head>
  <body>
    <button id="myButton">Colorize</button>
    <div
      id="myDiv"
      style="width: 300px; height: 200px;
background-color: red"
```

```html
></div>
<script>
  const myButton =
document.querySelector("#myButton");
  myButton.addEventListener("click", () =>
{
    const myDiv =
document.querySelector("#myDiv");
    myDiv.style.backgroundColor = "green";
  });
</script>
</body>
</html>
```

Colorize

Hello from the
scripts.js
scripts.js:1

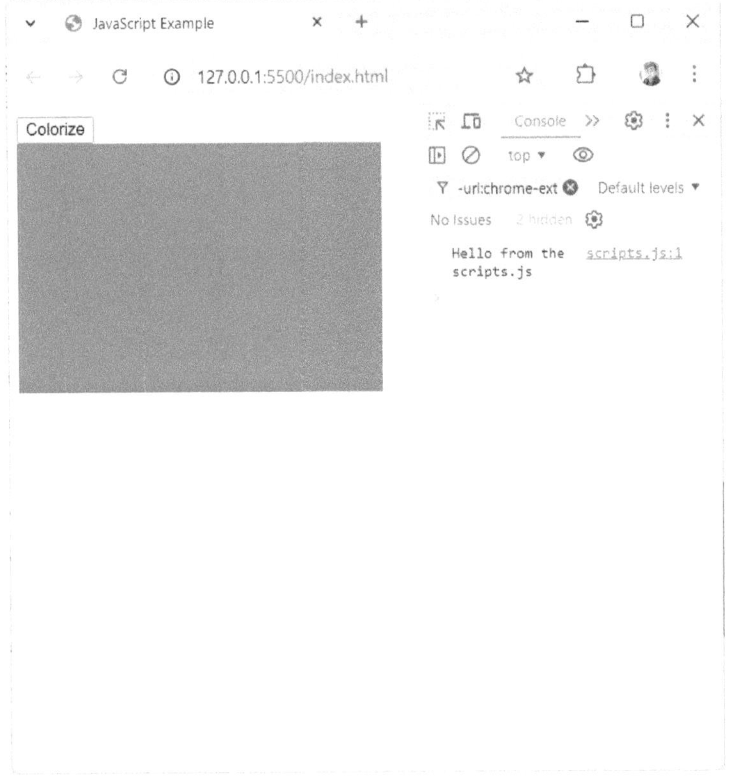


**Congratulations!** You have successfully completed your first JavaScript application in real life.

# What to do Next?

The aim of this book is to make it easier for you to get started with JavaScript. I have given you an overview of everything, but there are more details you will learn as you continue to work with JavaScript. Try to familiarise yourself with HTML and CSS and keep practicing JavaScript.

Do not try to create real applications using only JavaScript, because that will cost you a lot of time. Once you are confident with JavaScript and ready to build a real application, you should learn new JavaScript frameworks. I am talking about Angular, React and Vue. They all do the same thing, building client-side applications. In web development, there are two types of applications, server-side applications and client-side applications. The server-side applications are responsible for the business logic, security, database communication and so on, while the client-side applications are responsible for the user interface. They collect the user's input, send it to the backend server and display the results to the end user as soon as they are returned by the backend server. They do not perform sensitive operations such as security, business logic or communication with the database.

There are many programming languages for creating backend applications such as C#, Java, PHP, Node.JS (JavaScript), Python, etc.

For the frontend, it is mainly JavaScript and TypeScript with frameworks such as Angular, React and Vue.

Mobile applications are another type of application that are more similar to client-side applications and also connect to the backend server.

Most backend servers today are built on the principle of REST APIs. The server provides endpoints that the client can use to send and receive data.

You will learn everything over time, don't worry.

It may take you several attempts to understand a topic, so just keep going, because you will come across these topics again and again.

Over time, you will build up your understanding of the subject and approach things professionally.

Good luck with your learning and I will see you again on another topic!

— Abdelfattah Ragab

# Conclusion

**Congratulations!** You have read the book "JavaScript for Kids: Start Your Coding Adventure". Now you have a good understanding of JavaScript. Remember that learning JavaScript is an ongoing process. Practice makes perfect — build your own projects, experiment with the features you have learned, and delve into the extensive online resources.

Thank you for joining me in my exploration of JavaScript. I wish you the best of luck on your programming journey. Have fun programming and good luck with your applications!

# Media Attributions

Students working on computer laptops
Image by brgfx on Freepik

Modern annual report magazine page flyer a company catalog
Image by starline on Freepik

# Don't miss out!

Receive an email when Abdelfattah Ragab publishes a new book. It's free and without obligation.

# Also by Abdelfattah Ragab

◇ Angular for Kids

◇ CSS Flex Layout

◇ CSS Grid Layout

◇ CSS Box Model and Layouts

◇ Angular Portfolio App Development

# About the Author

Abdelfattah Ragab is a professional software developer with more than 20 years of experience.
https://abdelfattah-ragab.com

# About the Publisher

Abdelfattah Ragab is a highly qualified and experienced software developer with over 20 years of experience in the industry. Specializing in front-end development, Abdelfattah Ragab has a deep understanding of Angular, JavaScript, TypeScript, HTML and CSS. Read more at https://abdelfattah-ragab.com